Grade 2
Map Skills

Meeting Map Skill Standards with Exploratory Experiences

Written and Edited by
Alaska Hults

Illustrators: Mapping Specialists and Jenny Campbell
Cover Illustrator: Rick Grayson
Designer: Barbara Peterson
Cover Designer: Barbara Peterson
Art Director: Tom Cochrane
Project Director: Carolea Williams

Table of Contents

Introduction

The wonderful thing about teaching children map skills is that they really want to know how to read maps. To children maps are secret codes that any respectable spy must be able to figure out. Maps are keys to unknown places. Maps hold the promise of an adventure.

The learning standards at the second grade level are typically very simple. Second graders must

- understand that maps are representational.

- identify geographical features on a map.

- identify, locate, and use the map title, map key, compass rose, lines and borders, roads and routes, and objects and symbols.

- use grid systems to locate communities.

Use the maps and activity pages in *Map skills: Grade 2* to make your lessons fun and exploratory. Give children the maps, and read aloud the introductory text on the activity page. Have children discuss how the information relates to that map. Discuss with children the questions on the page, and have them work together to solve each problem or follow the directions to complete the tasks.

The maps in this resource progress from quite simple to more complex. Use them in order. Full lessons on each element are not provided. Supplement difficult concepts with lessons from your social studies curriculum. Schedule about 20 minutes for each map experience. Invite children to bring in maps they find, and have the class examine them. Have the class find the title, key or legend, scale, compass rose, and grid on the map.

Always invite the class to imagine what they could do with each map. The magic in a map is the possibility of new adventures. The skills children use will one day take them safely to the places they want to go. Conveniently, these skills will also transfer well to a standardized-testing situation.

How to Use This Book

Hitting the Map Standards

Before you have children read and complete the activity page that precedes each map, lay a firm foundation for the activity by having children complete the Evaluate the Map reproducible (page 5). This reproducible will keep children's map skills sharp for test-taking and will better prepare them to think critically as they complete the activity page that accompanies the map. Copy the map on an overhead transparency, and display it so you can point to specific elements of the map during discussion. You may want to use the tips that follow as you do so.

1. Have children work in pairs the first time they complete the reproducible. More details are identified when two pairs of eyes examine the same map.

2. Read the directions to the class. Have children take a moment to look at the map. If there are labels, invite volunteers to read them. Point to each label as it is read and have the rest of the class follow along. Be sure children understand what each label means before moving on. For example, when children look at the first map, you may have children find and count all the gas stations of apartment buildings.

3. Children may simply copy the title for question 1. For question 2 they should not repeat the information in the title. Have them carefully examine the map and say *This map was created by a person. What was the person trying to show or teach in this map?* Record responses on the board.

4. Children may need a thorough review of the map terms before they can complete question 3. Assign colors to each check box, and have children circle or underline parts of the map that correspond to each check box. Invite volunteers to do so on the overhead map.

5. Have children discuss their answers to question 4. Record their responses as a list on the board. When the discussion is complete, point to each word or phrase in the list and read it aloud. Then, encourage children to use the list to write a sentence that answers question 4. You may choose to have less fluent writers dictate their responses to you. Record their responses on an index card, and have them copy their answer onto the reproducible.

6. For question 5 invite children to simply jot down a keyword or words related to a part of the map that is confusing for them. Collect the reproducibles. Without reading names, quickly go through the reproducibles and read aloud the concerns. Use this information to clarify any areas of the map that are problematic for the class. You may spend more time on this step than on the others, but in return, children are likely to be much more independent as they complete the activity sheet that accompanies the map.

Name_____ **Date**_____

Evaluate the Map

Use the map to answer the questions.

1. The title is _____.

2. This map shows _____.

3. Check the box. This map has

    ❏ land and water.   ❏ a compass rose.

    ❏ a key.   ❏ grid lines.

    ❏ a scale.   ❏ latitude and /or longitude.

4. How could you use this map?

_____

_____

5. What does not make sense to you?

_____

_____

_____

Using the Activity Pages

Copy the map to an overhead transparency. Decide whether you are going to have children record their responses on the activity page or complete it orally. If you have children do their own work on the activity page, copy it and distribute one to each child. Display the map transparency. Give children time to review the features of the map, and then read aloud the instructional text on the activity page. Discuss and clarify any new terms. Have children look over the map, and discuss any confusing symbols or features of the map. Then, walk children through answering the questions or following the directions on the activity page. Have children respond verbally or record their responses on the activity page. Encourage frequent discussions as children work.

Special Notes

The first map focuses on two concepts only: that maps are shown from a bird's-eye-view and that each item on a map represents a real thing. For children who have strong spatial skills, the concept of bird's-eye-view needs almost no explanation. However, many children at this age still struggle with the concept. Try this quick activity to help them understand the concept. In advance, draw a few "blocks" on a large piece of construction paper. Use Monopoly® houses to assemble a simple "town." Have children pretend to be a bird and "fly" slowly over the town. Then, have them return to their seats and draw what they saw. Children may fly over the town more than once to recall all the items. Point out the similarities between their drawings and the first map on page 9.

Page 30 Create two 1¼" paper squares for each child. Use a pen to add three small marks that divide one side of each square into fourths and label each ¼ mi, ½ mi, ¾ mi, and 1 mi, respectively. Have children line up the edges of the square with the scale line to confirm that the length of the square equals 1 mile. Have them use the square to measure distances. Show children how to place the corner of the square on their starting location and line up the end location along the edge of the paper. Demonstrate how to use the small marks on the edge of the square to measure distance less than a mile (or, using two squares, a mile and some fraction of another mile). Some distances on this activity page do not require the use of the scale. Children should be able to determine more than and less than just by estimating the distances. To have children work in kilometers, work as above, but use a 3 cm square and divide one side into 1 km and ½ km using the marks on the scale.

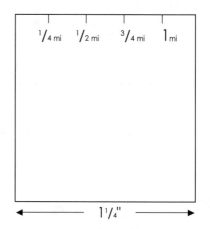

Build a map center. Laminate each map. You may want to make two copies of the map and put the answer key on the back of each map. Place the maps at the center with wipe-off markers and erasers. Provide additional atlases and at least one globe for children to examine.

- Have children compare the maps to each other. Do they all have titles? Do they all show the scale? How many of the maps have a grid? How are some of the symbols alike and different? What kinds of maps are easiest for them to read? Invite children to record their thoughts by jotting down key words in a map journal.

- Provide examples of simple and ornate compass roses. Provide long, thin paper triangles, glue, decorative items (e.g., sequins, feathers, and glitter), and a large piece of construction paper. Invite children to make their own compass rose. Have children label each direction on the compass.

- Provide die-cuts and large sheets of butcher paper. Invite children to make maps (suggest pirate maps, treasure maps, or maps that show how they get from home to school) using the die-cuts as symbols.

- Use Yarn to cover a large bulletin board with a 5-by-5 grid. Label the grid with index cards so that each column is numbered and each row is lettered. Place an index card labeled with a student name in each box. Obtain or create two large dice. Write a letter or number that matches the grid on each side of the die. For calling on volunteers, lining up to go to recess or lunch, or for choosing classroom responsibilities, roll each dice and match the letter and number that turn face-up to a name in the grid.

- Add grids to the maps that do not have them, and ask children to find certain items using the grid.

- Give each child a copy of three maps. Play "I Spy" with the class, having them locate the compass rose, the title, the scale, and small details in each map.

- Have children choose a favorite map. Ask them to create three quiz questions for that map, write each question on a slip of paper, and place the papers in a jar. At the end of the day, pull two questions from the jar, and have children determine which map contains the answer to the question. Then, have children find the answer to the question.

Name_____ Date_____

Our Town
Maps Show Places

Read.

Maps are pictures that show where things are. You could draw a map of your desk. You could draw a map of your house. You could draw a map of your town.

You read a map to get information. This map shows a neighborhood. If you needed to go to somewhere in the neighborhood, you could use the map to figure out how to get there.

Use the map to answer the questions.

1. How many restaurants are there in Our Town? _____

2. Which building shares a block with the park? _____

3. Find the apartment building next to the park. Move your finger to the right and find the restaurant that is on the same side of the street. If you walk from the apartment building to the restaurant on the same side of the street, how many houses will you pass?

   _____

4. How many gas stations are there in Our Town? _____

5. What kind of building is represented by the book symbol?

   _____

6. In this town, a gas station is always near a _____ and _____ .

Map Skills: Grade 2 © 2005 Creative Teaching Press

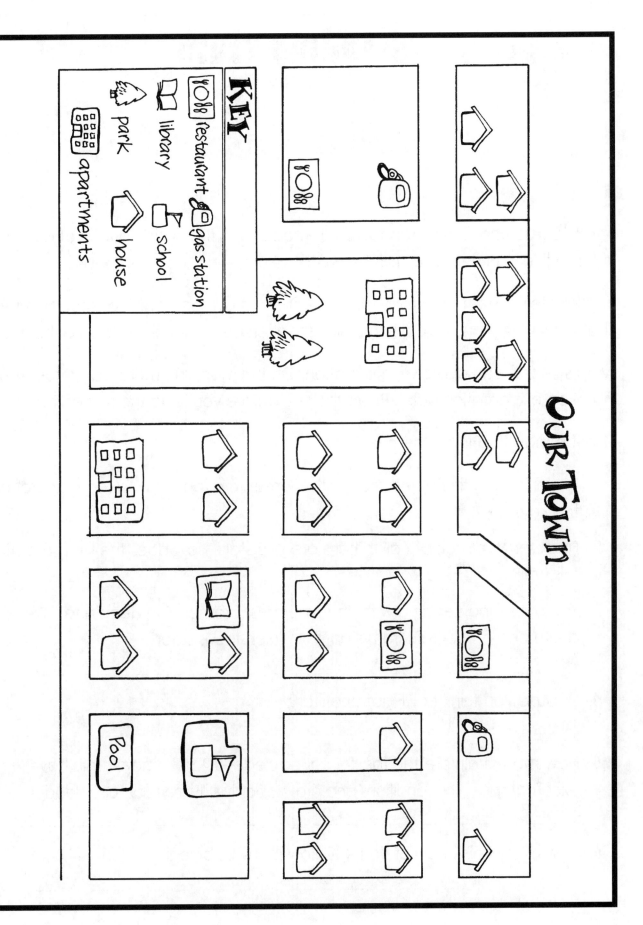

Our Town

KEY

restaurant
gas station
library
school
park
house
apartments

Map Skills: Grade 2 © 2005 Creative Teaching Press

Sledding Trails
Title and Key

Read.

The **title** tells what the map shows. This map shows the sledding trails of a popular hill. The title can help you find the map you need in a book of maps.

The **key** tells what the map symbols mean. Map symbols can be small pictures that show where one object is. A black dot often means there is a town in that place.

Map symbols can also give information. On this map, the more dangerous routes have an exclamation point. Read the key before you read the rest of the map.

Use the map to answer the questions.

1. Underline the title of the map with a green crayon. Draw a red box around the key.

2. Find start #4. Look at trail I. There are two stars. How does the map describe this trail? _____

3. You are going sledding with your youngest brother. You decide to take him down one of the trails from start #1. Which trail is safer?

   _____

4. Why do you think trail F got one star?

   _____

5. How many trails are too fast for young sledders? How many trails have excellent speed or conditions and are probably still safe for young sledders?

   _____   _____

6. How many trails begin at start #3? How many trails begin at start #4?

   _____   _____

Map Skills: Grade 2 © 2005 Creative Teaching Press

Sledding Trails

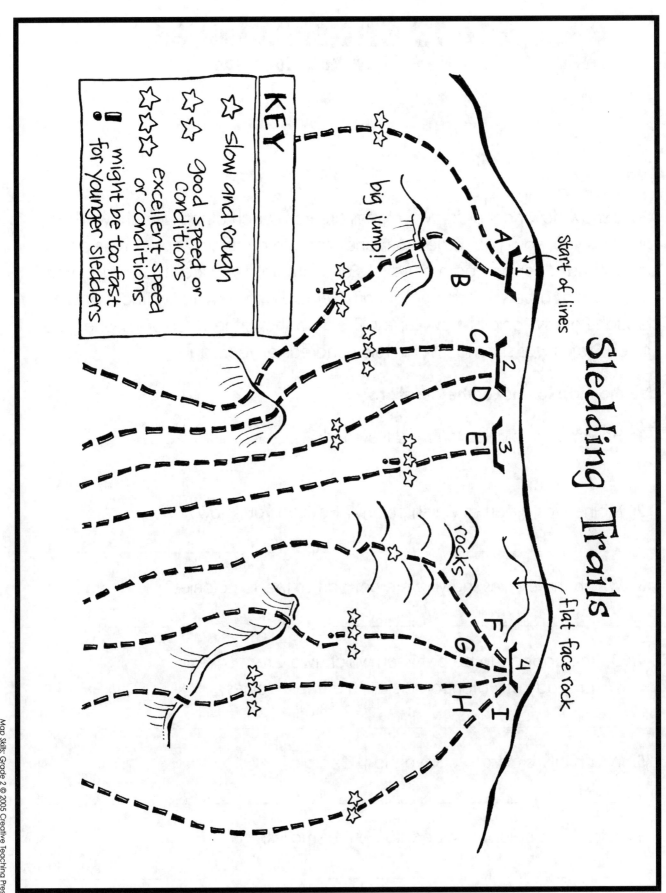

KEY

☆ slow and rough

☆☆ good speed or
conditions

☆☆☆ excellent speed
or conditions

▮ might be too fast

● for younger sledders

Start of lines

big jump!

A
B
1

C D
2

E
3

rocks

flat face rock

F
G
H I
4

Map Skills: Grade 2 © 2005 Creative Teaching Press

The 13 British Colonies
Maps Show Relationships

Read.

Maps show how near or far two places are from each other. They show what direction you would go to get from one place to another. Maps can help you understand a person's path of travel. For example, if you look at this map you can see that a person cannot get from Delaware to New York without passing through Pennsylvania or New Jersey. This map shows the 13 colonies when the United States was still under British rule hundreds of years ago.

Use the map to answer the questions.

1. How many colonies touched New York? _____

2. Maine was a part of which colony? How do you know?

   _____

3. Which three cities shown were not part of the 13 colonies?

   _____

4. Detroit appears to be between which two Great Lakes?
   Which body of water borders all 13 of the colonies?

   _____   _____

5. Which city is closest to Savannah, Georgia?

   _____

6. Which two colonies appear to be the smallest?

   _____

Map Skills: Grade 2 © 2005 Creative Teaching Press

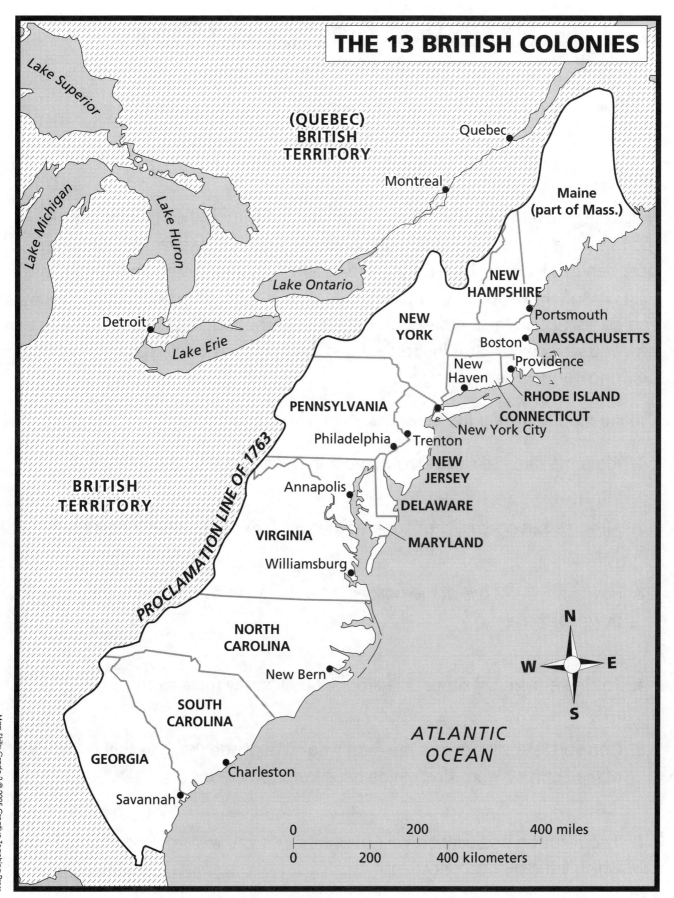

THE 13 BRITISH COLONIES

Lake Superior

Lake Michigan

Lake Huron

Lake Ontario

Lake Erie

Detroit

(QUEBEC) BRITISH TERRITORY

Quebec

Montreal

Maine (part of Mass.)

NEW HAMPSHIRE

Portsmouth

NEW YORK

Boston

MASSACHUSETTS

New Haven

Providence

RHODE ISLAND

PENNSYLVANIA

CONNECTICUT

New York City

Philadelphia

Trenton

NEW JERSEY

BRITISH TERRITORY

DELAWARE

Annapolis

MARYLAND

VIRGINIA

Williamsburg

NORTH CAROLINA

New Bern

SOUTH CAROLINA

GEORGIA

Charleston

Savannah

ATLANTIC OCEAN

PROCLAMATION LINE OF 1763

N
W   E
S

0		200		400 miles
0	200		400 kilometers	

Happyland Amusement Park
Birds-Eye View

Read.

Maps only show the most important information. This map shows where the restrooms and restaurants are located. It does not show where every trash can and park bench is located. Pretend you are visiting Happyland Amusement Park with your parents. How would you plan to spend the day at this park? Where would you go first? Read the key first so that you know what each symbol means. This is how you would know that the rattle shows the place to go to if you lost your parents and needed help finding them.

Use the map to answer the questions.

1. There are three services located near the eating area. What are they?

   _____ _____ _____

2. After the bus goes by the Slippery Slide which two rides does it pass next?

   _____ _____

3. How many ATMs are at the park? In how many places can you rent a stroller or wheelchair?

   _____ _____

4. Are there more gift shops or restrooms? How many more?

   _____ _____

5. Can you tell by looking at the map what kind of ride the Ride to the Center of the Earth is? What kind of ride is the Whoop-de-Loop?

   _____ _____

6. If you tripped and skinned your knee badly as you were getting off The Drop, which first aid station is closest? _____

Map Skills: Grade 2 © 2005 Creative Teaching Press

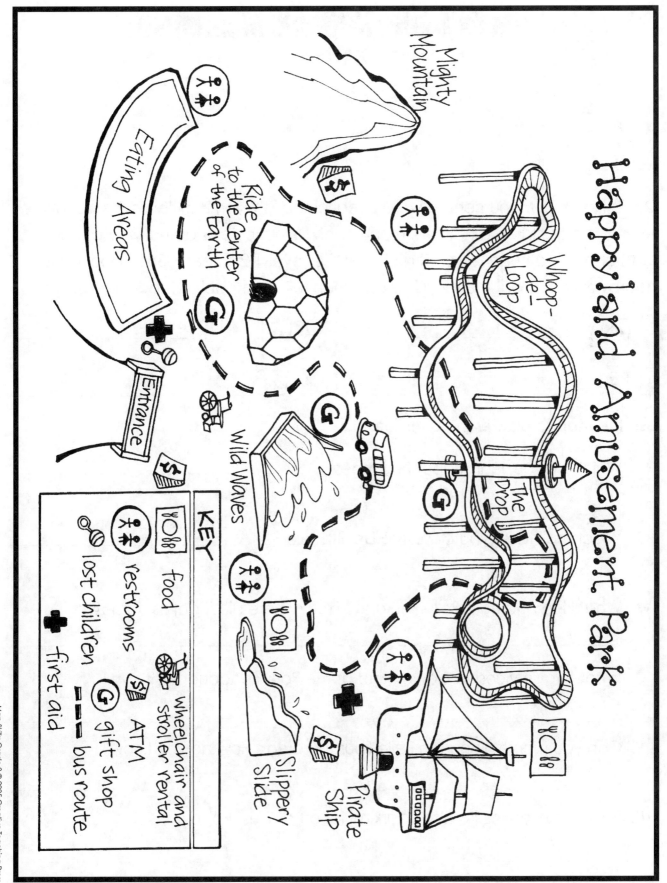

Name_____ Date_____

Devils Tower National Monument
Review

Read.

Devils National Monument Tower is a real place in Wyoming. It was the first place ever to be declared a national monument. Devils Tower is actually a natural landform. It is a huge tower of rock that rises over 1,200 feet (386m) above the nearby river. Look at the map key and then tell what each symbol means.

1. [△] _____   2. [⛏] _____

3. [🏕] _____   4. [🚻] _____

Use the map to answer the questions.

5. Which trail appears to be the longest? _____

6. Which trail takes you closest to Devils Tower? _____

7. What kind of area is Belle Fourche? From where did it get its name?

_____   _____

8. What two services would you find at the Park Headquarters?

_____   _____

9. Can you picnic along the Belle Fourche area? How do you know?

_____   _____

10. Which trail leaves from the parking lot off of West Road?

_____

Map Skills: Grade 2 © 2005 Creative Teaching Press

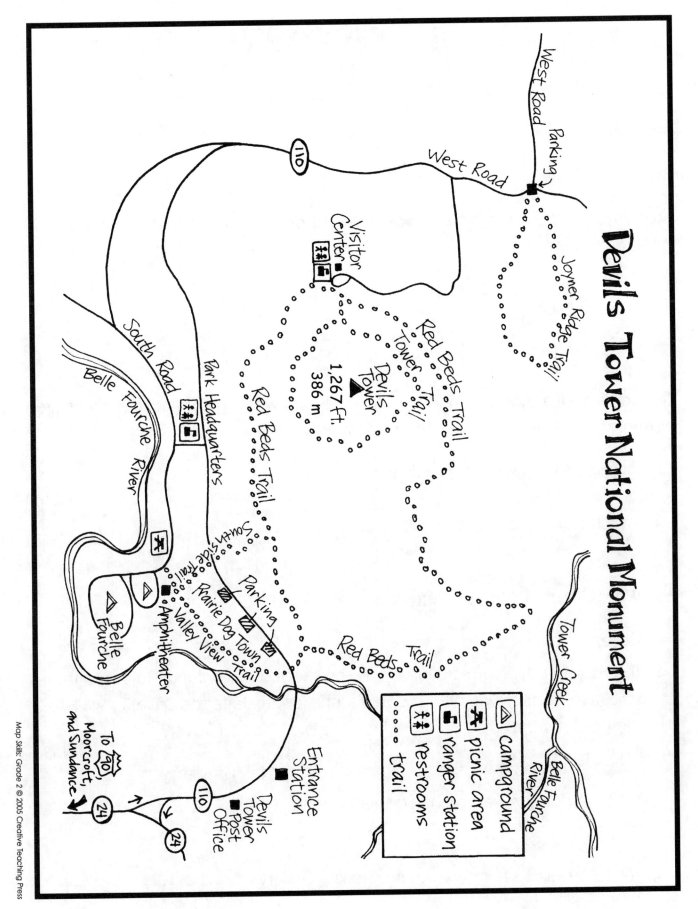

Devils Tower National Monument

West Road Parking

West Road

Joyner Ridge Trail

110

Visitor Center

Red Beds Trail

Tower Trail

Devils Tower

1,267 ft.
386 m

Red Beds Trail

South Road

Belle Fourche River

Park Headquarters

South Side Trail

Prairie Dog Town

Parking

Red Beds Trail

Tower Creek

Belle Fourche River

Belle Fourche

Amphitheater

Valley View Trail

To Moorcroft, and Sundance

24

110

24

Entrance Station

Devils Tower Post Office

110

○○○○ trail

👥 restrooms

🏠 ranger station

⛽ picnic area

⛺ campground

Map Skills: Grade 2 © 2005 Creative Teaching Press

The Smithsonian
The Compass Rose

Read.

Maps show direction with a **compass rose**. A compass rose tells which way is north on the map.

Simple   **Detailed**

The **cardinal directions** are north, south, east, and west. The **ordinal directions** are northeast, northwest, southeast, and southwest.

Use the map to answer the questions.

1. Which building is farthest east? _____

2. Which two buildings are farthest north?

   _____ _____

3. The Hirshhorn Museum is a large building shaped like a donut. To get to the sculpture garden, you go through a tunnel under Jefferson Drive. To walk to the garden from the museum, which direction do you travel?

   _____

4. Which building is west of the Sackler Gallery? _____

5. Which building is northwest of the Sackler Gallery? _____

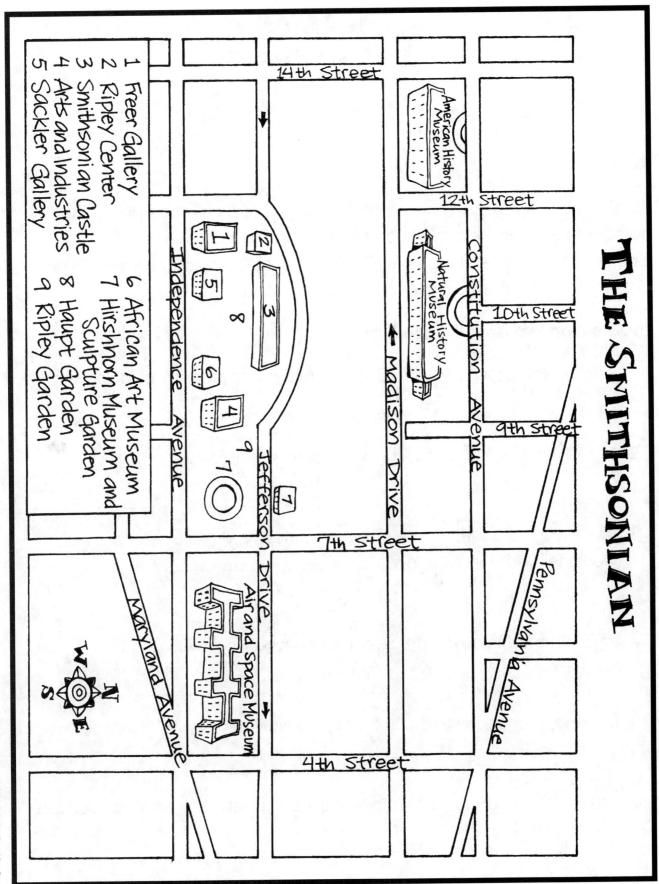

THE SMITHSONIAN

Map Key

1 Freer Gallery
2 Ripley Center
3 Smithsonian Castle
4 Arts and Industries
5 Sackler Gallery
6 African Art Museum
7 Hirshhorn Museum and Sculpture Garden
8 Haupt Garden
9 Ripley Garden

14th Street
12th Street
10th Street
9th Street
7th Street
4th Street

American History Museum
Natural History Museum
Air and Space Museum

Independence Avenue
Jefferson Drive
Madison Drive
Constitution Avenue
Pennsylvania Avenue
Maryland Avenue

N W E S

Map Skills: Grade 2 © 2005 Creative Teaching Press

The Co-op
Letters and Numbers

Read.

Letters and numbers can be useful in finding places on a map. Look at the numbered rows on the map. Trace them across the map with your finger. Find each numbered aisle of the store. On this map, at the place where row B meets aisle 4, you will find sweets, bread flour, and soy flour.

Use the map to answer the questions.

1. If you went to row 2, section C, which two kinds of foods would you find?

   _____ _____

2. Name the food items you would find across all of row A.

   _____

3. If you wanted to get a cart to do your shopping, which row and aisle would tell you where to go? _____

4. If you wanted to buy some cereal, which aisle would you go to?

   _____

5. It is time to check out. Which row do you walk to?

   _____

6. You want to feed your family a dinner of bean burritos tonight. Which sections do you go to?

   _____

Map Skills: Grade 2 © 2005 Creative Teaching Press

The Co-Op

A
B
C
D

cereal   bread

Vegetables

Meat and Eggs

Dairy

Checkout

1

salt   sugar   flour

canned vegetables

2

soup   pasta

tortillas   salsa   beans

3

spices   condiments

chips   cookies   sweets

4

Bulk Items

honey   almond butter   peanut butter   soy flour   bread flour   whole wheat flour

Map Skills: Grade 2 © 2005 Creative Teaching Press

La Crosse, Wisconsin
Using a Grid and Index

Read.

A **grid** is used on many maps to help break up the area into smaller pieces. Then you can use the pieces to find places. You usually say the letter first and then the number.

Most road maps use a grid and an **index** to help you find places. An index is a list of important places on the map and the letter and number of the piece of the map where they can be found.

Use the map and index to answer the questions.

Western Wisconsin Technical College	**C2**
Wisconsin Travel Information Center	**B1**
Grandad Bluff	**C3**
State Office Building	**D2**

1. If you added both hospitals to the index, what letter and number would tell their location? _____

2. What important place is at A1? _____

3. If you drive north from the State Office Building and keep going north after you pass Western Wisconsin Technical College, what squares will you pass through before you hit the edge of the map?

_____

4. What small town is northeast of La Crosse, in A3? _____

5. What major river runs through most of Column 1? _____

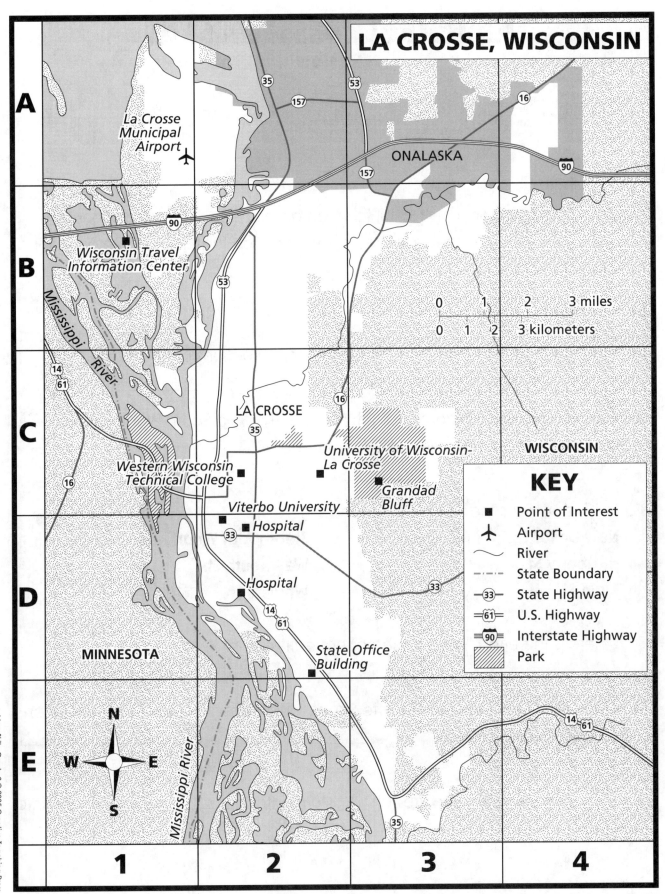

LA CROSSE, WISCONSIN

A

La Crosse
Municipal
Airport ✈

35 53 157 16

ONALASKA

157 90

B

90

Wisconsin Travel
Information Center

53

Mississippi River

0   1   2   3 miles
0 1 2 3 kilometers

C

14
61

16

LA CROSSE

35

16

University of Wisconsin-
La Crosse

WISCONSIN

Western Wisconsin
Technical College

Viterbo University

Grandad
Bluff

KEY

■ Point of Interest
✈ Airport
∿ River
–·– State Boundary
—33— State Highway
=61= U.S. Highway
≡90≡ Interstate Highway
▨ Park

D

Hospital

33

Hospital

33

14
61

MINNESOTA

State Office
Building

E

N
W   E
S

Mississippi River

14 61

35

1   **2**   **3**   **4**

Nantucket, Massachusetts
Review

Read.

This is a simple road map of a small town on a small island near Massachusetts. Many of the streets are one-way streets. The direction that it is legal to drive in is shown by the arrows on the map.

Use the map to answer the questions.

1. Which symbol can you use to figure out the directions on the map?

   _____

2. Can you drive south from Straight Wharf (B4) to Old South Wharf (B4) on Candle Street? If not, how can you get there?

   _____

3. The index gives the following information:

New Dollar Ln.	D2		Steamboat Wharf	A4
N. Liberty St.	B1		Weymouth St.	D5
Main St.	C1–B3		Whalers Ln.	A3

   Where is the error? What is the correct entry?

   _____   _____

4. If you drive southwest on Fayette Street, which direction must you turn when you get to Union Street? _____

5. If you drive east on Milk Street (D1), it turns into _____ in C2 and then into _____ in B1.

Map Skills: Grade 2 © 2005 Creative Teaching Press

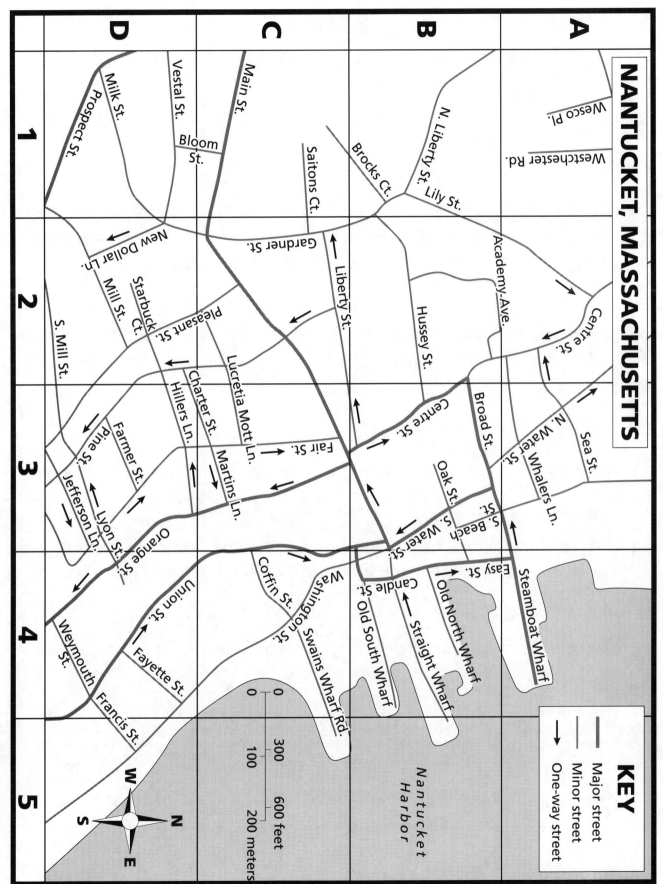

NANTUCKET, MASSACHUSETTS

KEY

Major street
Minor street
One-way street

Nantucket Harbor

300   600 feet
100   200 meters
0

N
W E
S

Map Skills: Grade 2 © 2005 Creative Teaching Press

Egypt
Hemispheres, Latitude, and the Equator

Read.

Look at a globe. A globe includes imaginary lines that help people locate places a lot like the grid does. The **equator** is an imaginary line that divides the globe into a northern and southern half. These halves are called **hemispheres**.

The imaginary lines that go around the earth above and below the equator are called **latitude** lines. These lines are numbered in degrees. The higher the number, the closer it is to the north or south pole. The lower the number, the closer it is to the equator.

Use the map to answer the questions.

1. There are three lines of latitude shown on this map. How are they numbered?

   _____ _____ _____

2. The "N" stands for the hemisphere in which that line of latitude is found. Is Egypt in the Northern Hemisphere or Southern Hemisphere?

   _____

3. Does the line at 32°N go through any part of Egypt? What does it cross through?

   _____

4. Which of the lines of latitude does the Nile River cross?

   _____

5. Is the capital city north or south of 28°N? _____

6. Which city sits exactly on 24°N? _____

Map Skills: Grade 2 © 2005 Creative Teaching Press

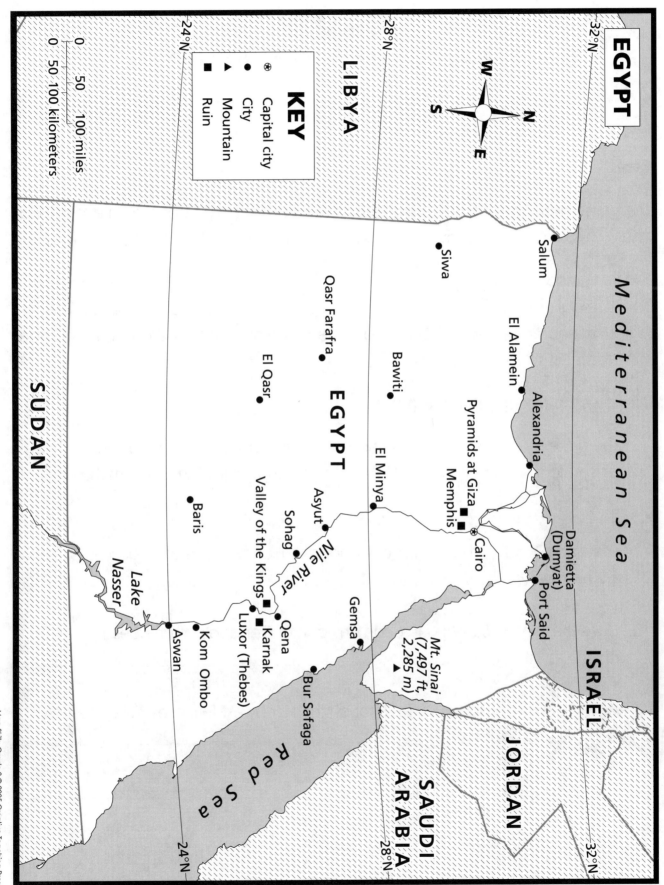

EGYPT

Mediterranean Sea

KEY
⊛ Capital city
● City
▲ Mountain
■ Ruin

N
W E
S

LIBYA

SUDAN

EGYPT

ISRAEL

JORDAN

SAUDI ARABIA

Red Sea

Salum

Siwa

Qasr Farafra

Bawiti

El Qasr

El Minya

El Alamein

Alexandria

Pyramids at Giza
Memphis

Cairo ⊛

Damietta (Dumyat)

Port Said

Asyut

Sohag

Valley of the Kings

Nile River

Gemsa

Baris

Lake Nasser

Aswan

Kom Ombo

Luxor (Thebes)

Karnak

Qena

Bur Safaga

Mt. Sinai
(7,497 ft,
2,285 m) ▲

0   50   100 kilometers
0   50   100 miles

24°N
28°N
32°N

Map Skills: Grade 2 © 2005 Creative Teaching Press

Canada
Longitude and the Prime Meridian

Read.

The **prime meridian** is an imaginary line that divides the globe into an eastern half and a western half. You may remember that these halves are called hemispheres.

The imaginary lines that go around the earth from the North Pole to the South Pole are called **longitude** lines. These lines are also numbered in degrees. The higher the number, the farther it is from the prime meridian. The lower the number, the closer it is to the prime meridian.

Use the map to complete the activities.

1. There are many lines of longitude shown on this map. Which line of longitude is closest to the prime meridian? Which line of longitude is farthest from the prime meridian? _____   _____

2. Use the key to find the capital of Canada. Which two lines of longitude is it between? _____   _____

3. Does the line at 150°W go through any part of Canada? What does it cross through? _____

4. Which line of longitude crosses through the Northwest Territories, Yukon Territory, and British Columbia? _____

5. Is Winnipeg east or west of 90°W? _____

6. Through which waters does 140°W pass?

_____

Map Skills: Grade 2 © 2005 Creative Teaching Press

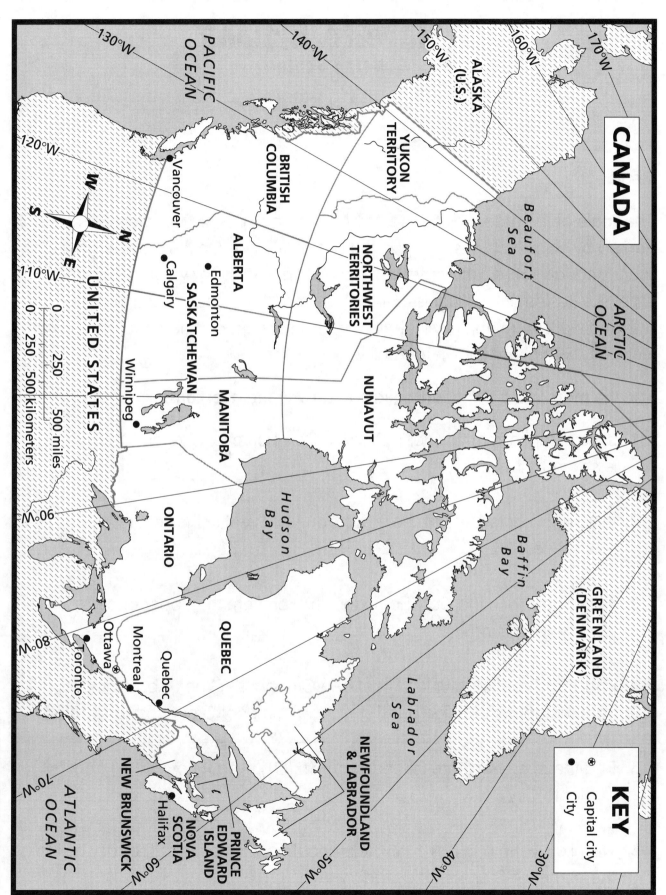

CANADA

KEY

⊗ Capital city
● City

ALASKA (U.S.)

YUKON TERRITORY

BRITISH COLUMBIA

NORTHWEST TERRITORIES

NUNAVUT

ALBERTA

● Edmonton
● Calgary

SASKATCHEWAN

MANITOBA

● Winnipeg

ONTARIO

● Vancouver

UNITED STATES

QUEBEC

Ottawa ⊗
● Montreal
● Quebec
● Toronto

NEWFOUNDLAND & LABRADOR

NEW BRUNSWICK

NOVA SCOTIA

PRINCE EDWARD ISLAND

● Halifax

PACIFIC OCEAN

ARCTIC OCEAN

Beaufort Sea

Baffin Bay

Hudson Bay

Labrador Sea

ATLANTIC OCEAN

GREENLAND (DENMARK)

130°W
140°W
150°W
160°W
170°W
120°W
110°W
90°W
80°W
70°W
60°W
50°W
40°W
30°W

N
S
E
W

0   250   500 miles
0   250   500 kilometers

Lafayette, Indiana
Using Scale

Read.

The **scale** of the map is a line that tells how many miles or kilometers are represented by each inch. It is usually in the bottom corner. On this map, every 1¼" inches equals 1 mile. Lafayette, Indiana is a fairly small city when compared to cities like Boston or Los Angeles. Still, it is an important place to the people who live and work there. This city in the heart of America is also home to an excellent university with a well-known football team.

Use the map and a 1¼" paper square to answer the questions.

1. Is the distance from City Hall (C2) to the Cary Home for Children (D3) more or less than 1 mile? _____

2. Which is closer to City Hall: the hospital on 14th Street or the hospital on South Street? _____

3. About how far is the Cary Home for Children from the Tippecanoe County Fairgrounds? _____

4. Find 18th Street. Find Union Street and Greenbush Street. About how far is it from the corner of Union and 18th to the corner of Greenbush and 18th?
_____

5. Find the corner of State St. and Grant St. (C1). About how far is it from this corner to City Hall? _____

6. West Lafayette also has a city hall. About how far is it from that city hall to the corner of Grant St. and Stadium Ave. (C1)? _____

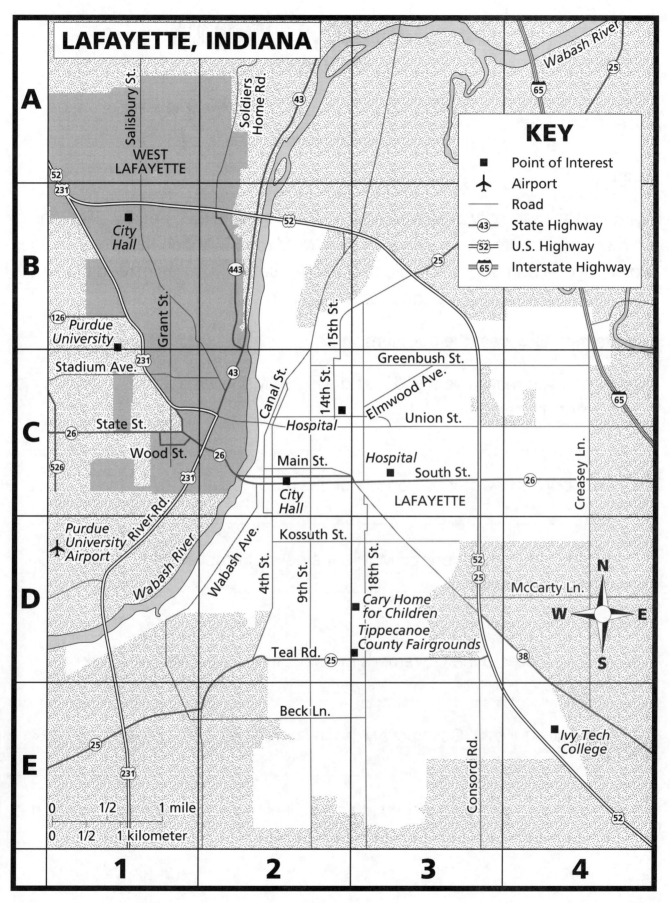

LAFAYETTE, INDIANA

KEY

- ■ Point of Interest
- ✈ Airport
- — Road
- –43– State Highway
- =52= U.S. Highway
- 65 Interstate Highway

WEST LAFAYETTE

Salisbury St.

Soldiers Home Rd.

City Hall

Grant St.

Purdue University

Stadium Ave.

State St.

Wood St.

Canal St.

15th St.

14th St.

Greenbush St.

Elmwood Ave.

Union St.

Hospital

Hospital

Main St.

City Hall

South St.

LAFAYETTE

Creasey Ln.

Kossuth St.

Purdue University Airport

Wabash River

River Rd.

Wabash Ave.

4th St.

9th St.

18th St.

Cary Home for Children

Tippecanoe County Fairgrounds

McCarty Ln.

Teal Rd.

Beck Ln.

Consord Rd.

Ivy Tech College

Wabash River

N
W E
S

0   1/2   1 mile

0   1/2   1 kilometer

A B C D E

1 2 3 4

Map Skills: Grade 2 © 2005 Creative Teaching Press

Sacramento, California
Review

Read.

This map shows the city of Sacramento, California. Highways, nearby cities, and points of interest are shown. This is a simple road map that can help you find your way from one part of Sacramento to the other. Before you begin, read the key, notice the scale of the map, and use the compass rose to find north.

Use the map to answer the questions.

1. Tell how you know which road is a state highway and which is an interstate highway.

   _____

2. What bodies of water do you see on this map? _____

   _____

3. If you drove from Arden Fair Mall to the nearest hospital, which direction would you travel? _____

4. Which is closer to the Governor's Mansion, the Zoo or Discovery Park?

   _____

5. About how far is the Governor's Mansion from Sutter's Fort State Historical Park?

   _____

6. If the State Capitol building and museum is the center of Sacramento, in which direction would you travel to get to Fruitridge? _____

Map Skills: Grade 2 © 2005 Creative Teaching Press

SACRAMENTO, CALIFORNIA

99

5

Canal

Canal

Sacramento River

Canal

■ ARCO Arena

Canal

80

80

Del Paso Park ■

BR 80

80

Discovery Park ■

American River

160

Arden Fair Mall ■

Hospital ■

80

● Bryte

California Highway Patrol Academy ■

Broderick ●

Governor's Mansion ■

SACRAMENTO

California Exposition ■

Arden ●

BR 80

Sutter's Fort State Historical Park ■

Hospital ■

California State University- Sacramento

80

Port of Sacramento ■

West Sacramento

State Capitol & Museum ■

BR 80

Deep Water Ship Canal

5

160

99

50

Hospital ■

16

N
W ✦ **E**
S

Zoo ■

Fruitridge ●

Morrison River

Lake Greenhaven

160

Florin Mall ■

Florin ●

Parkway ■

Southgate Plaza ■

99

Sacramento River

Freeport ●

5

0	1	2 miles
0	1	2 kilometers

KEY

● City

■ Point of Interest

〜 River

—160— State Highway

═50═ U.S. Highway

═5═ Interstate Highway

Map Skills: Grade 2 © 2005 Creative Teaching Press

Sri Lanka
Review

Read.

Sri Lanka is a small island off the coast of India in the Northern and Eastern Hemispheres.

Before you begin, read the map key, notice the scale of the map, and use the compass rose to find north.

Use the map to answer the questions.

1. What does a triangle represent on this map? _____

2. What is the capital of Sri Lanka? _____

3. How can you tell the difference between the land and water on this map?

   _____

4. There are five different kinds of bodies of water on this map.
   There are rivers, a strait, a bay, a _____, and an _____.

5. Which city is the farthest north on the island? _____

6. About how far is it from Kurunegala to Maho? _____

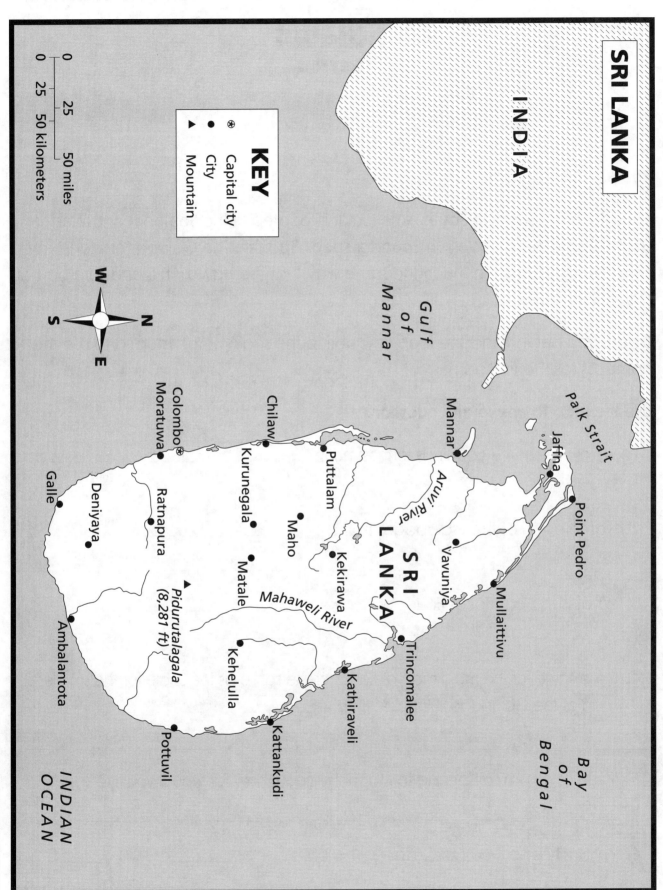

SRI LANKA

INDIA

Gulf
of
Mannar

Palk Strait

Bay
of
Bengal

KEY
⊗ Capital city
● City
▲ Mountain

W N
S E

0 25 50 miles
0 25 50 kilometers

Mannar
Jaffna
Point Pedro
Vavuniya
Mullaittivu
Aruvi River
S R I
L A N K A
Trincomalee
Kathiraveli
Kattankudi
Pottuvil
Kehelulla
Mahaweli River
Kekirawa
Matale
▲ Pidurutalagala
(8,281 ft)
Maho
Puttalam
Kurunegala
Ratnapura
Deniyaya
Chilaw
Colombo ⊗
Moratuwa
Galle
Ambalantota

INDIAN
OCEAN

Map Skills: Grade 2 © 2005 Creative Teaching Press

Ecuador
Review

Read.

Ecuador is a country in South America. It is located in the Southern and Western Hemispheres. Most people in Ecuador speak Spanish. The Galapagos Islands are also part of Ecuador in much the same way that the Hawaiian Islands are part of the United States.

Before you begin, read the map key, notice the scale of the map, and use the compass rose to find north.

Use the map to answer the questions.

1. Which river in the country is farthest north? _____

2. Name each of the Galapagos Islands. _____

_____ _____ _____

3. What is the capital of Ecuador? _____

4. Is the scale for the main map of Ecuador the same as the scale for the smaller map of the Galapagos Islands? _____

5. If you flew from La Libertad to Machala, about how far would you fly?

_____

6. What city is northeast of Quito? _____

Map Skills: Grade 2 © 2005 Creative Teaching Press

ECUADOR

GALAPAGOS ISLANDS

Isabela
San Salvador
Santa Cruz
San Cristobal

0   50   100 miles
0   50   100 kilometers

PACIFIC OCEAN

W   N
S   E

0   50   100 miles
0   50   100 kilometers

La Libertad

Gulf of Guayaquil

Manta

Machala

Babahoyo

Chone

ECUADOR

Rosa Zarate

Esmeraldas

San Lorenzo

COLOMBIA

⊗ Quito

Ambato

Tena

Tulcan

Ibarra

Zamora

Macas

Pastaza River

Rio Tigre

Cononaco

Napo River

PERU

KEY
⊗ Capital city
● City

Map Skills: Grade 2 © 2005 Creative Teaching Press

Portland, Oregon
Review

Read.

This is a road map of Portland, Oregon. Be sure to read the key before you begin.

Use the map to answer the questions.

1. What is the name of the river that goes through D2 and E3?

   _____

2. Which cities would you find at D1? _____

3. Which city is closer to Gladstone: Clackamas or West Linn?

   _____

4. If you live in Wilsonville (E1), which interstate highway would take you to Vancouver, Washington (A2)? _____

5. If you live in Raleigh Hills and travel east and then north on Highway 10, which U.S. highway would you come to first? _____

6. When you cross the Columbia River, you enter a new state. What is it?

   _____

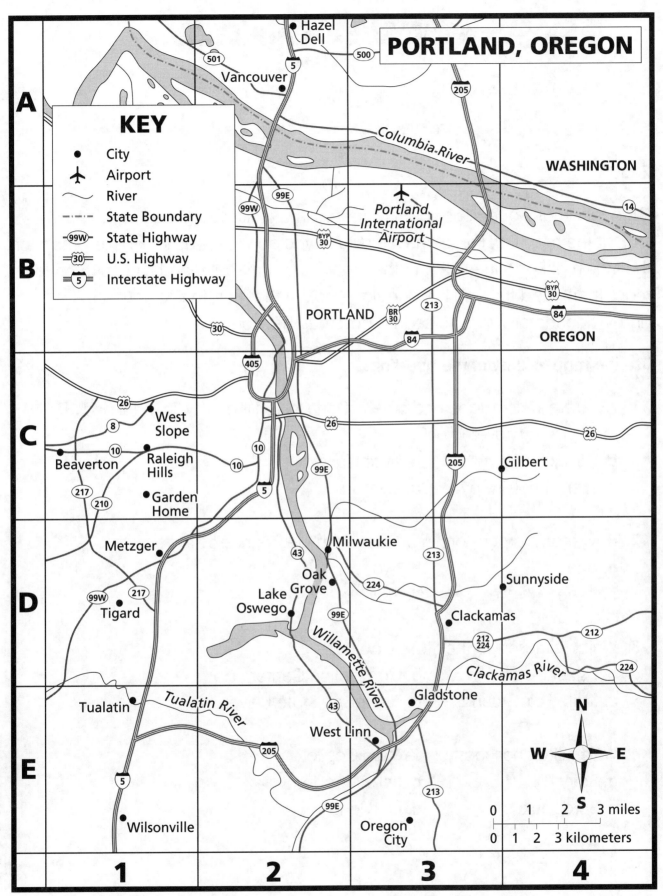

PORTLAND, OREGON

KEY

- • City
- ✈ Airport
- ～ River
- –·–·– State Boundary
- ⊂99W⊃ State Highway
- ⊂30⊃ U.S. Highway
- ⊂5⊃ Interstate Highway

Hazel Dell

Vancouver

Columbia River

WASHINGTON

Portland International Airport

PORTLAND

OREGON

West Slope

Beaverton

Raleigh Hills

Garden Home

Gilbert

Metzger

Milwaukie

Sunnyside

Oak Grove

Lake Oswego

Tigard

Clackamas

Willamette River

Clackamas River

Tualatin

Tualatin River

Gladstone

West Linn

Wilsonville

Oregon City

N
W E
S

0   1   2   3 miles

0   1   2   3 kilometers

A B C D E

1 2 3 4

Nashville, Tennessee
Review

Read.

On a test, many questions about maps are in a multiple-choice format. Always look at the map first. Follow the same rules you do when you look at any map for the first time. Read the title and the key, look at the scale, and find north on the map. Then, read through the question. Look at the map to find your answer. Finally, find the answer choice that best matches your answer.

Use the map to answer the questions.

1. If you live in Hermitage and drive to Donelson on Highway 70, what kind of road are you traveling on?
   a. U.S. Highway   **b.** State Highway
   c. Interstate Highway   **d.** Railroad

2. How many airports are in or near Nashville, Tennessee?
   a. one   **b.** two
   c. three   **d.** four

3. Which is closest to the State Capitol?
   a. Fisk University   **b.** Convention Center
   c. State Fair Grounds   **d.** Tennessee State University

4. Which city is northeast of the State Capitol?
   a. Berry Hill   **b.** Belle Meade
   c. Bordeaux   **d.** Opryland

Map Skills: Grade 2 © 2005 Creative Teaching Press

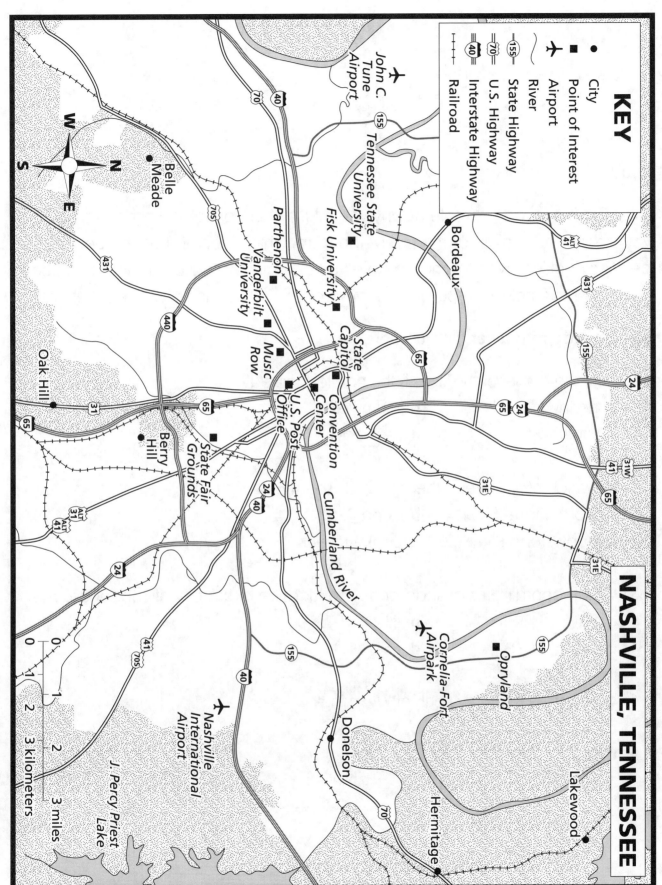

KEY

- City
- Point of Interest
- Airport
- River
- State Highway
- U.S. Highway
- Interstate Highway
- Railroad

NASHVILLE, TENNESSEE

John C. Tune Airport

Belle Meade

Tennessee State University

Fisk University

Parthenon

Vanderbilt University

Music Row

State Capitol

U.S. Post Office

Convention Center

Bordeaux

Oak Hill

Berry Hill

State Fair Grounds

Cumberland River

Cornelia-Fort Airpark

Oryland

Lakewood

Donelson

Hermitage

Nashville International Airport

J. Percy Priest Lake

0 1 2 3 miles

0 1 2 3 kilometers

Map Skills: Grade 2 © 2005 Creative Teaching Press

Wyoming
Review

Read.

This map is a good example of why you might want to look over the map before you begin. The scale is at the top of the map, which is an unusual place for it to be. Also, looking over the map before you begin gives you a chance to notice details. For example, did you notice that Wyoming is surrounded by six other states?

Use the map to answer the questions.

1. In which corner of the state is the capital located?
   a. northwest   **b.** southwest
   c. southeast   **d.** northeast

2. By which major river is the city of Casper (C4) located?
   a. North Platte River   **b.** Wind River
   c. Yellowstone River   **d.** Snake River

3. Which coordinates best describe the location of the city of Sundance?
   a. A1   **b.** B1
   c. D5   **d.** B5

4. Which state is directly north of Wyoming?
   a. South Dakota   **b.** Montana
   c. Colorado   **d.** Idaho

Map Skills: Grade 2 © 2005 Creative Teaching Press

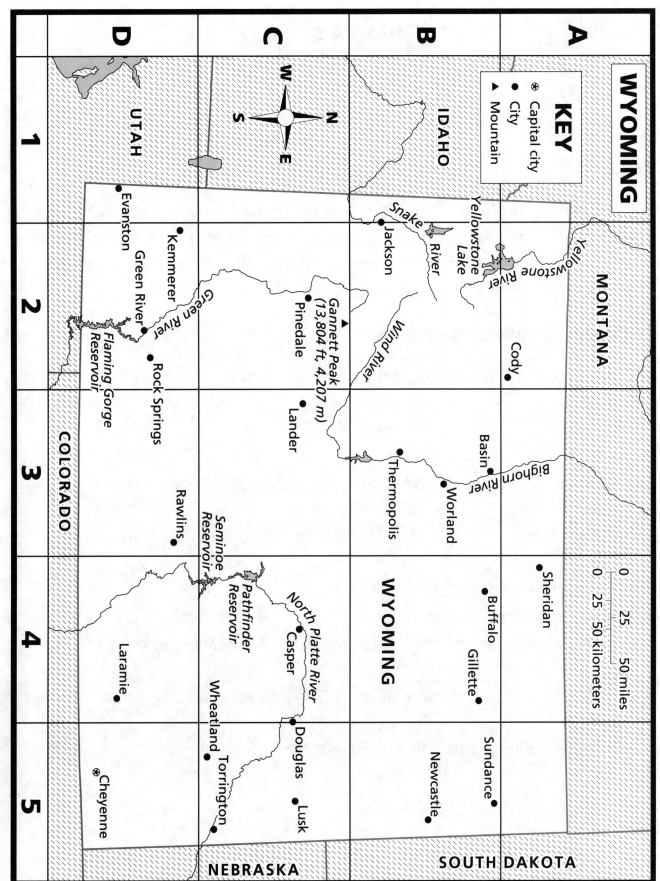

WYOMING

KEY
⊛ Capital city
● City
▲ Mountain

MONTANA

IDAHO

UTAH

COLORADO

NEBRASKA

SOUTH DAKOTA

WYOMING

Yellowstone Lake

Yellowstone River

Snake River

Wind River

Bighorn River

Green River

Flaming Gorge Reservoir

Seminoe Reservoir

Pathfinder Reservoir

North Platte River

Gannett Peak
(13,804 ft, 4,207 m)

● Evanston
● Kemmerer
● Green River
● Rock Springs
● Pinedale
● Lander
● Rawlins
● Jackson
● Cody
● Basin
● Thermopolis
● Worland
● Sheridan
● Buffalo
● Gillette
● Sundance
● Newcastle
● Laramie
● Casper
● Douglas
● Lusk
● Wheatland
● Torrington
⊛ Cheyenne

N W E S

0   25   50 miles
0 25 50 kilometers

Map Skills: Grade 2 © 2005 Creative Teaching Press

United States

Read.

Do you live in any of the places shown on this map? Even if you think you have seen a place mapped out before, you should look carefully at the map. Two different maps of the United States might show very different features based on what the mapmaker thought was important.

Use the map to answer the questions.

1. How many different scales are shown on this map?
   a. three   **b.** two
   c. one   **d.** none

2. Which river runs along the border between Texas and Oklahoma?
   a. Platte River   **b.** Ohio River
   c. Red River   **d.** Mississippi River

3. Which states border Lake Michigan?
   a. Wisconsin and Michigan   **b.** Michigan and Ohio
   c. Michigan, Indiana, Illinois, and Wisconsin   **d.** Minnesota and Wisconsin

4. About how far is it from Washington, D.C. to Atlanta, Georgia?
   a. 250 mi or 500 km   **b.** 550 mi or 875 km
   c. 750 mi or 1,000 km   **d.** 500 mi or 500 km

Map Skills: Grade 2 © 2005 Creative Teaching Press

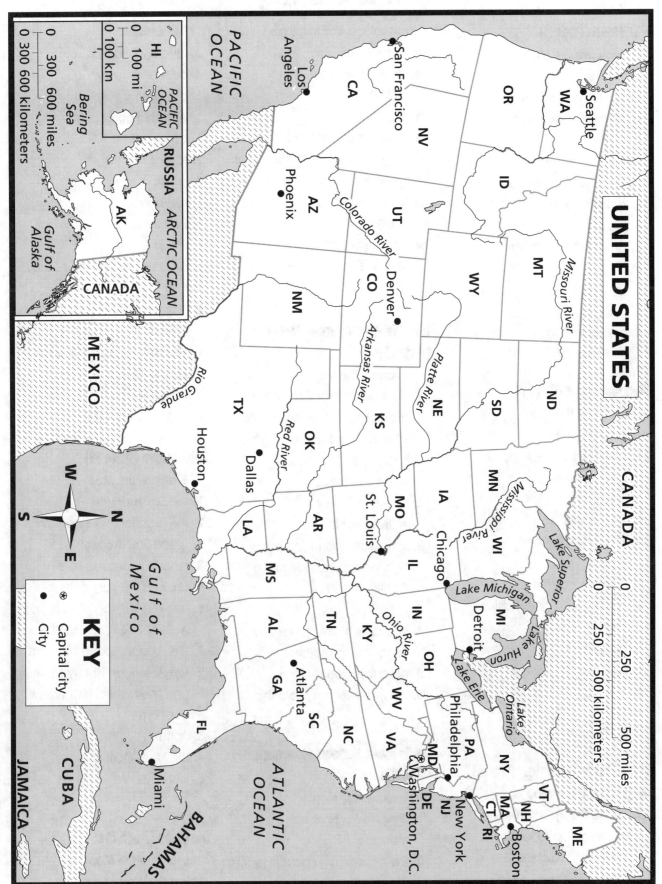

UNITED STATES

KEY
⊛ Capital city
• City

CANADA

MEXICO

Inset map
HI

PACIFIC OCEAN

RUSSIA
ARCTIC OCEAN
AK
Bering Sea
Gulf of Alaska
CANADA

Scale:
0 100 mi
0 100 km

0 300 600 miles
0 300 600 kilometers

PACIFIC OCEAN

WA · Seattle
OR
ID
MT
Missouri River
ND
SD
NE
Platte River
WY
CA
San Francisco ·
· Los Angeles
NV
UT
Colorado River
AZ
· Phoenix
CO
Denver ⊛
NM
Arkansas River
Rio Grande
TX
· Dallas
Houston ·
OK
Red River
KS
St. Louis ·
MO
AR
LA
MS
AL
Atlanta ·
GA
FL
· Miami

Gulf of Mexico

CUBA
JAMAICA
BAHAMAS
ATLANTIC OCEAN

MN
IA
WI
Mississippi River
IL
Chicago ·
IN
MI
Detroit ·
Lake Superior
Lake Michigan
Lake Huron
Lake Erie
Lake Ontario
Ohio River
KY
TN
OH
WV
VA
NC
SC
PA
Philadelphia ·
MD
Washington, D.C. ⊛
DE
NJ
New York ·
NY
VT
NH
MA
CT
RI
Boston ·
ME

Compass: N E S W

Map Skills: Grade 2 © 2005 Creative Teaching Press

Answer Key

Our Town (Page 9)
Evaluate the Map
1. Our Town
2. the kinds of buildings in Our Town and where they are
3. a key
4. answers will vary
5. answers will vary

Activity Page
1. 3
2. an apartment building
3. 3
4. 2
5. a library
6. house; restaurant

Sledding Trails (Page 11)
Evaluate the Map
1. Sledding Trails
2. where each sledding trail is and how dangerous it is
3. a key
4. answers will vary
5. answers will vary

Activity Page
1. Check student work.
2. good speed or conditions
3. trail A
4. because it goes over rocks so it is slow and bumpy
5. 3; 2
6. 1; 4

The 13 British Colonies (Page 13)
Evaluate the Map
1. the 13 British Colonies
2. the names and locations of the British Colonies
3. land and water, a key,

a scale, a compass rose
4. answers will vary
5. answers will vary

Activity Page
1. 5
2. Massachusetts; Mass. is an abbreviation for Massachusetts
3. Detroit, Montreal, Quebec
4. Lake Huron and Lake Erie; the Atlantic Ocean
5. Charleston, South Carolina
6. Rhode Island and Delaware

Happyland Amusement Park (Page 15)
Evaluate the Map
1. Happyland Amusement Park
2. the location of important places at Happyland Amusement Park
3. a key
4. answers will vary
5. answers will vary

Activity Page
1. first aid, restrooms, lost parents
2. Wild Waves and Ride to the Center of the Earth
3. 3; 1
4. restrooms; there is one more restroom than gift shops
5. no; a rollercoaster
6. the one near the Pirate ship

Devils Tower National Monument (Page 17)
Evaluate the Map
1. Devils Tower National Monument
2. the location of important places at Devils Tower National

Monument
3. land and water, a key
4. answers will vary
5. answers will vary

Activity Page
1. campground
2. ranger station
3. picnic area
4. restrooms
5. Red Beds Trail
6. Tower Trail
7. a campground; the nearby river
8. restrooms and the ranger station
9. Yes, there is a picnic area symbol by the river
10. Joyner Ridge Trail

Smithsonian (Page 19)
Evaluate the Map
1. the Smithsonian
2. the location of key buildings at the Smithsonian
3. a key, a compass rose
4. answers will vary
5. answers will vary

Activity Page
1. the Air and Space Museum
2. the American History Museum and the Natural History Museum
3. north
4. the Freer Gallery
5. Ripley Cente

The Co-op (Page 21)
Evaluate the Map
1. The Co-op

2. the location of food items at a small food co-op
3. none
4. answers will vary
5. answers will vary

Activity Page

1. canned vegetables and pasta
2. vegetables, meat, eggs, and dairy
3. 4D
4. aisle 1
5. row D
6. 3B and 3C

La Crosse, Wisconsin (Page 23)

Evaluate the Map

1. La Crosse, Wisconsin
2. the location of key places in and around La Crosse, WI
3. land and water, a key, a scale, compass rose, grid lines
4. answers will vary
5. answers will vary

Activity Page

1. D2
2. the La Crosse Municipal Airport
3. D2, C2, B2, and A2
4. Onalaska, Wisconsin
5. The Mississippi River

Nantucket, Massachusetts (Page 25)

Evaluate the Map

1. Nantucket, Massachusetts
2. important roads of Nantucket, MA
3. land and water, a key, scale,

a compass rose, grid lines
4. answers will vary
5. answers will vary

Activity Page

1. the compass rose
2. no; you have to go to S. Water St. to get there
3. Weymouth St.; D4
4. You must go right, which is northwest.
5. Gardner St.; N. Liberty St. or Lily St.

Egypt (Page 27)

Evaluate the Map

1. Egypt
2. important cities of Egypt
3. land and water, a key, a scale, compass rose, grid lines (latitude)
4. answers will vary
5. answers will vary

Activity Page

1. 24°N, 28°N, 32°N
2. the Northern Hemisphere
3. no; Libya, the Mediterranean Sea, Jordan, and Israel
4. 24°N and 28°N
5. north
6. Aswan, Egypt

Canada (Page 29)

Evaluate the Map

1. Canada
2. important cities of Canada
3. land and water, a key, a scale, a compass rose, grid lines (longitude)
4. answers will vary

5. answers will vary

Activity Page

1. 30°W; 170°W
2. 70°W and 80°W
3. no; Alaska, which is part of the United States
4. 130°W
5. west
6. the Arctic Ocean, Beaufort Sea, and Pacific Ocean

Lafayette, Indiana (Page 31)

Evaluate the Map

1. Lafayette, Indiana
2. important places in Lafayette, IN
3. land and water, a key, a scale, a compass rose, grid lines
4. answers will vary
5. answers will vary

Activity Page

1. more than
2. the hospital on 14th Street
3. about 1/3 mi, a little over 1/2km
4. about 1/2 mi, a little over 3/4 km
5. a little over 1 mi., 1³/₄ km
6. about 1¹/₃ mi, 2¹/₄ km

Sacramento, California (Page 33)

Evaluate the Map

1. Sacramento, California
2. important places in Sacramento, CA
3. land and water, a key, a scale, a compass rose
4. answers will vary
5. answers will vary

Activity Page

1. The state highway number is in an oval and is one gray line. The Interstate highway number is in a shield with a dark top and is three lines.
2. the American River, Port of Sacramento, Deep Water Ship Canal, Sacramento River, Lake Greenhaven, Morrison River, and smaller canals that run through the city
3. east
4. Discovery Park
5. about 1 mi, about 1¹/₂ km
6. southeast

Sri Lanka (Page 35)

Evaluate the Map

1. Sri Lanka
2. important cities of Sri Lanka
3. land and water, a key, a scale, a compass rose
4. answers will vary
5. answers will vary

Activity Page

1. a mountain
2. Colombo
3. The water is gray and the land is white or hatch-marked.
4. gulf; ocean
5. Point Pedro
6. 25 mi, 40 km

Ecuador (Page 37)

Evaluate the Map

1. Ecuador
2. important cities of Ecuador
3. land and water, a key, a scale,

a compass rose

4. answers will vary
5. answers will vary

Activity Page

1. the Napo River
2. Isabela, San Salvador, Santa Cruz, and San Cristobal
3. Quito
4. no
5. ~100 mi, ~160 km
6. Ibarra

Portland, Oregon (Page 39)

Evaluate the Map

1. Portland, Oregon
2. important places in Portland, OR
3. land and water, a key, a scale, a compass rose, grid lines
4. answers will vary
5. answers will vary

Activity Page

1. the Willamette River
2. Metzger and Tigard
3. West Linn
4. Highway 5
5. Highway 26
6. Washington

Nashville, Tennessee (Page 41)

Evaluate the Map

1. Nashville, Tennessee
2. important places in Nashville, TN
3. land and water, a key, a scale, a compass rose
4. answers will vary
5. answers will vary

Activity Page

1. a
2. c
3. b
4. d

Wyoming (Page 43)

Evaluate the Map

1. Wyoming
2. important cities of Wyoming
3. land and water, a key, a scale, a compass rose, grid lines
4. answers will vary
5. answers will vary

Activity Page

1. c
2. a
3. d
4. b

United States (Page 45)

Evaluate the Map

1. The United States
2. important places in the United States
3. land and water, a key, a scale, a compass rose
4. answers will vary
5. answers will vary

Activity Page

1. a
2. c
3. c
4. b